# SCHIRMER'S LIBRARY
## OF MUSICAL CLASSICS

Vol. 2104

# FRÉDÉRIC CHOPIN

# The Ultimate Piano Collection

Complete Ballades, Études, Mazurkas, Nocturnes,
Polonaises, Préludes, and Waltzes

ISBN 978-1-4803-3278-2

# G. SCHIRMER, Inc.

DISTRIBUTED BY

HAL•LEONARD®
CORPORATION
7777 W. BLUEMOUND RD. P.O. BOX 13819 MILWAUKEE, WI 53213

www.musicsalesclassical.com
www.halleonard.com

# Contents

## Ballades

## Études

## Mazurkas

*(continued)*

# Nocturnes

# Polonaises

# Préludes

# Waltzes

# BALLADES

*à Monsieur le Baron de Stockhausen*

# BALLADE
in G minor

Frédéric Chopin
Op. 23

* In some editions:
In manchen Ausgaben:

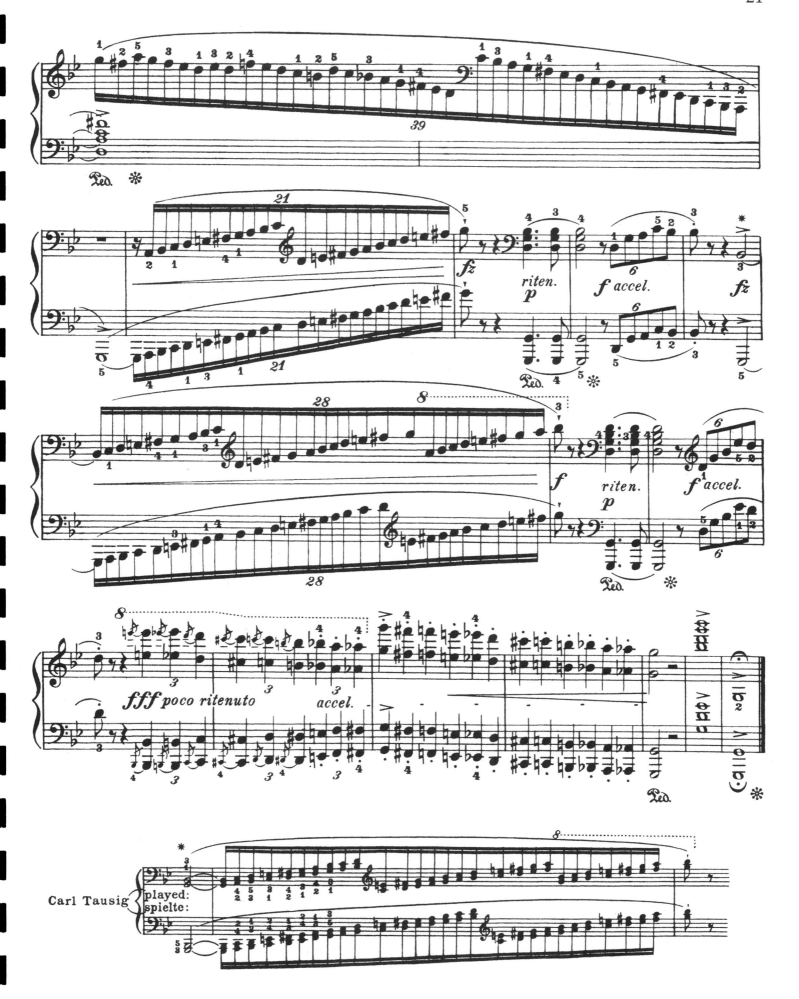

*à Robert Schumann*

# BALLADE
in F Major

Frédéric Chopin
Op. 38

Presto con fuoco

26

Tempo I°

Presto con fuoco

30

*à Mademoiselle de Noailles*

# BALLADE
## in A-flat Major

Frédéric Chopin
Op. 47

* In the Kullak Edition:
* In der Kullak-Ausgabe:

*à Madame la Baronne C. de Rothschild*

# BALLADE
## in F minor

Frédéric Chopin
Op. 52

*) The upper fingering, without the 3d finger, is for small hands.
*) Der obere Fingersatz, ohne den 3ten finger, für kleinere Hände.

Or:
Oder:

Or, as facilitated:
Oder zur Erleichterung:

# ÉTUDES

*à F. Liszt*

# ÉTUDE
## in C Major

Frédéric Chopin
Op. 10, No. 1

*à F. Liszt*

# ÉTUDE
### in A minor

Frédéric Chopin
Op. 10, No. 2

à F. Liszt

# ÉTUDE
in E Major

Frédéric Chopin
Op. 10, No. 3

à F. Liszt

# ÉTUDE
in C-sharp minor

Frédéric Chopin
Op. 10, No. 4

*à F. Liszt*

# ÉTUDE
## in G-flat Major

Frédéric Chopin
Op. 10, No. 5

à F. Liszt

# ÉTUDE
in E-flat minor

Frédéric Chopin
Op. 10, No. 6

*à F. Liszt*

# ÉTUDE
in C Major

Frédéric Chopin
Op. 10, No. 7

*à F. Liszt*

# ÉTUDE
## in F Major

Frédéric Chopin
Op. 10, No. 8

*à F. Liszt*

# ÉTUDE

in F minor

Frédéric Chopin
Op. 10, No. 9

*à F. Liszt*

# ÉTUDE
in A-flat Major

Frédéric Chopin
Op. 10, No. 10

*à F. Liszt*

# ÉTUDE
in E-flat Major

Frédéric Chopin
Op. 10, No. 11

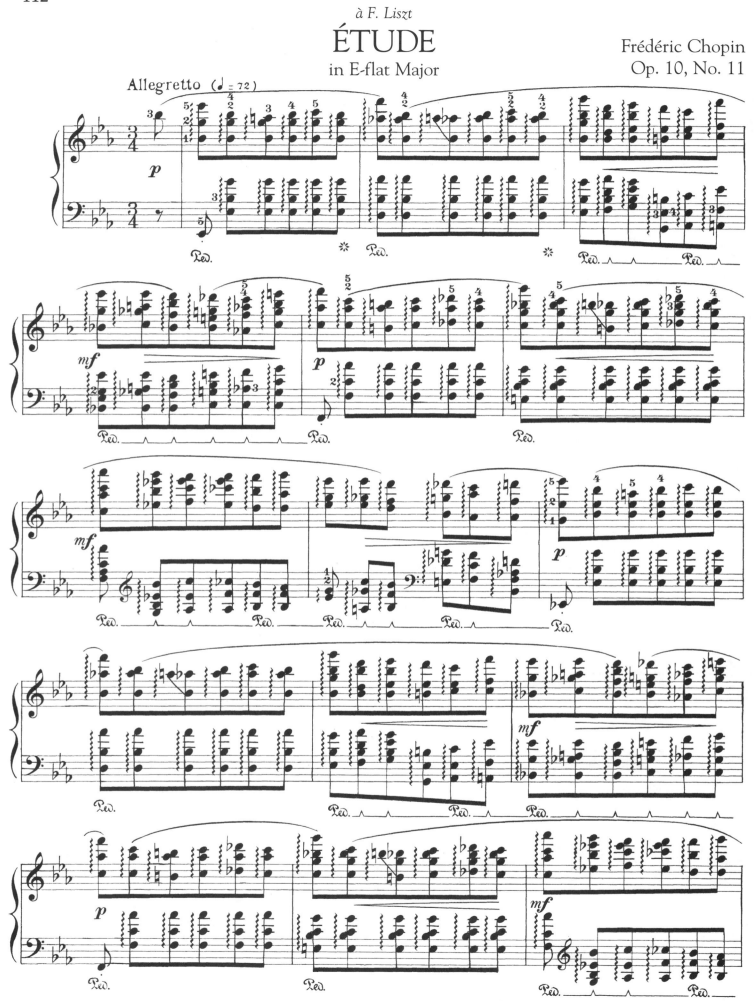

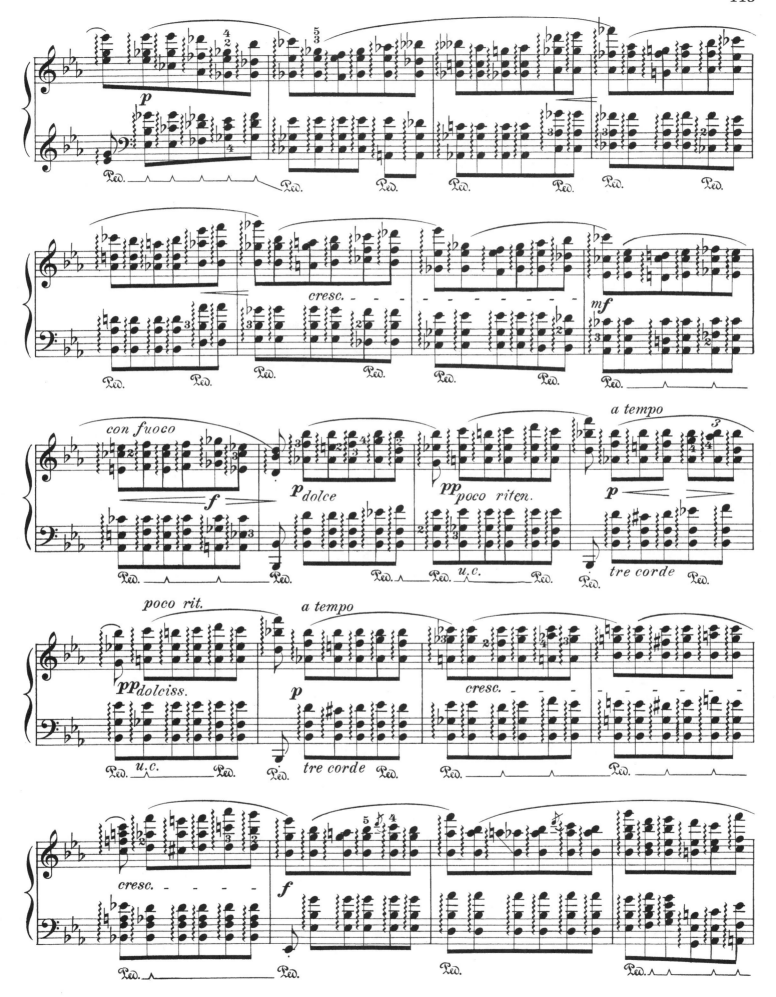

*à F. Liszt*

# ÉTUDE
## in C minor

**Frédéric Chopin**
Op. 10, No. 12

Allegro con fuoco ( ♩ = 144 )

*à Madame la Comtesse d'Agoult*

# ÉTUDE
## in A-flat Major

Frédéric Chopin
Op. 25, No. 1

*à Madame la Comtesse d'Agoult*

# ÉTUDE
in A minor

Frédéric Chopin
Op. 25, No. 4

*à Madame la Comtesse d'Agoult*

# ÉTUDE
## in F minor

Frédéric Chopin
Op. 25, No. 2

Presto ($\textstyle\frac{1}{2}$ = 112)

*à Madame la Comtesse d'Agoult*

# ÉTUDE
## in F Major

Frédéric Chopin
Op. 25, No. 3

*à Madame la Comtesse d'Agoult*

# ÉTUDE
in E minor

Frédéric Chopin
Op. 25, No. 5

*à Madame la Comtesse d'Agoult*

# ÉTUDE

in G-sharp minor

Frédéric Chopin
Op. 25, No. 6

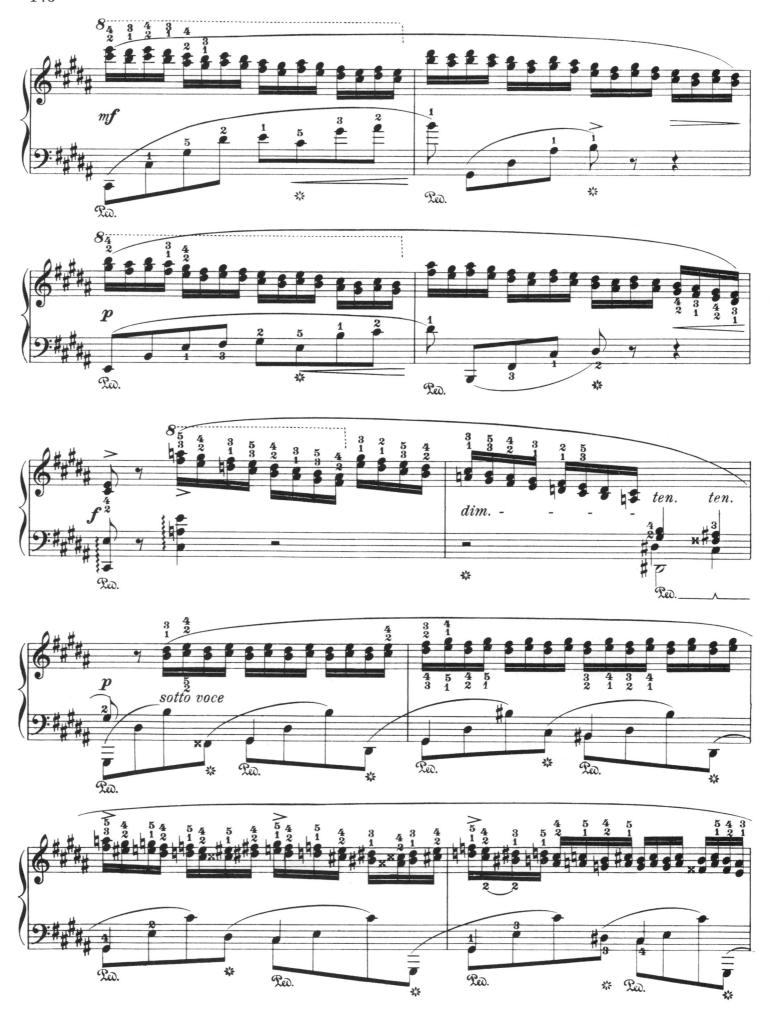

*à Madame la Comtesse d'Agoult*

# ÉTUDE
## in C-sharp minor

Frédéric Chopin
Op. 25, No. 7

*à Madame la Comtesse d'Agoult*

# ÉTUDE
## in D-flat Major

Frédéric Chopin
Op. 25, No. 8

Vivace legato (♩ = 80)

*à Madame la Comtesse d'Agoult*

# ÉTUDE
## in G-flat Major

Frédéric Chopin
Op. 25, No. 9

*à Madame la Comtesse d'Agoult*

# ÉTUDE
### in B minor

Frédéric Chopin
Op. 25, No. 10

Allegro con fuoco (♩ = 60)

Tempo I°

*à Madame la Comtesse d'Agoult*

# ÉTUDE
### in A minor

Frédéric Chopin
Op. 25, No. 11

*à Madame la Comtesse d'Agoult*

# ÉTUDE
## in C minor

Frédéric Chopin
Op. 25, No. 12

Allegro molto, con fuoco (♩ = 76)

# TROIS NOUVELLES ÉTUDES

from *Méthode des méthodes de piano*

### Étude in F minor

Frédéric Chopin

# Étude in A-flat Major

Frédéric Chopin

# Étude in D-flat Major

Frédéric Chopin

# MAZURKAS

*à Mademoiselle la Comtesse Pauline Plater*

# MAZURKA
in F-sharp minor

Frédéric Chopin
Op. 6, No. 1

*à Mademoiselle la Comtesse Pauline Plater*

# MAZURKA
### in C-sharp minor

Frédéric Chopin
Op. 6, No. 2

à Mademoiselle la Comtesse Pauline Plater

# MAZURKA
in E Major

Frédéric Chopin
Op. 6, No. 3

*à Mademoiselle la Comtesse Pauline Plater*

# MAZURKA

in E-flat minor

Frédéric Chopin
Op. 6, No. 4

*à Monsieur Johns de la Nouvelle-Orléans*

# MAZURKA

in B-flat Major

Frédéric Chopin
Op. 7, No. 1

*à Monsieur Johns de la Nouvelle-Orléans*

# MAZURKA
## in A minor

Frédéric Chopin
Op. 7, No. 2

à Monsieur Johns de la Nouvelle-Orléans

# MAZURKA
### in F minor

Frédéric Chopin
Op. 7, No. 3

Tempo I

con forza

rubato

à Monsieur Johns de la Nouvelle-Orléans

# MAZURKA
## in C Major

Frédéric Chopin
Op. 7, No. 5

Dal Segno senza Fine

*à Monsieur Johns de la Nouvelle-Orléans*

# MAZURKA
## in A-flat Major

Frédéric Chopin
Op. 7, No. 4

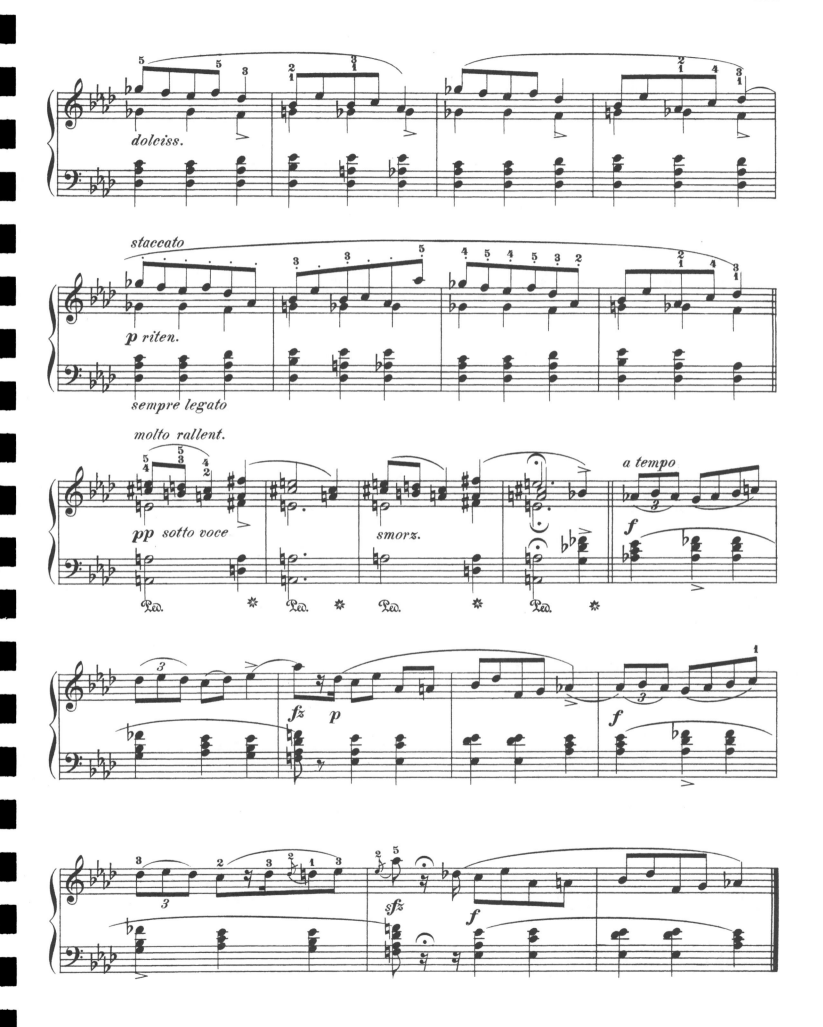

à Mademoiselle Lina Freppa

# MAZURKA

in B-flat Major

Frédéric Chopin
Op. 17, No. 1

**Vivo e risoluto** (♩ = 160)

*à Mademoiselle Lina Freppa*

# MAZURKA
### in E minor

Frédéric Chopin
Op. 17, No. 2

Lento, ma non troppo (♩ = 144)

*à Mademoiselle Lina Freppa*

# MAZURKA
in A-flat Major

Frédéric Chopin
Op. 17, No. 3

à Mademoiselle Lina Freppa

# MAZURKA
in A minor

Frédéric Chopin
Op. 17, No. 4

*à Monsieur le Comte de Perthuis*

# MAZURKA

in G minor

Frédéric Chopin
Op. 24, No. 1

*à Monsieur le Comte de Perthuis*

# MAZURKA
## in C Major

Frédéric Chopin
Op. 24, No. 2

*à Monsieur le Comte de Perthuis*

# MAZURKA
in A-flat Major

Frédéric Chopin
Op. 24, No. 3

*à Monsieur le Comte de Perthuis*

# MAZURKA

in B-flat minor

Frédéric Chopin
Op. 24, No. 4

*à la Princess de Würtemburg*

# MAZURKA

in C minor

Frédéric Chopin
Op. 30, No. 1

**Allegro non tanto**

*à la Princess de Würtemburg*

# MAZURKA
## in B minor

Frédéric Chopin
Op. 30, No. 2

*à la Princess de Würtemburg*

# MAZURKA

in D-flat Major

Frédéric Chopin
Op. 30, No. 3

*à la Princess de Würtemburg*

# MAZURKA
in C-sharp minor

Frédéric Chopin
Op. 30, No. 4

*à Mademoiselle la Comtesse Mostowska*

# MAZURKA
in G-sharp minor

Frédéric Chopin
Op. 33, No. 1

*à Mademoiselle la Comtesse Mostowska*

# MAZURKA
## in D Major

Frédéric Chopin
Op. 33, No. 2

*à Mademoiselle la Comtesse Mostowska*

# MAZURKA
## in C Major

Frédéric Chopin
Op. 33, No. 3

*à Mademoiselle la Comtesse Mostowska*

# MAZURKA
## in B minor

Frédéric Chopin
Op. 33, No. 4

*à Monsieur Etienne Witwicki*

# MAZURKA
## in E minor

Frédéric Chopin
Op. 41, No. 1

**Andantino**

*à Monsieur Etienne Witwicki*

# MAZURKA
### in B Major

Frédéric Chopin
Op. 41, No. 2

*à Monsieur Etienne Witwicki*

# MAZURKA
### in A-flat Major

Frédéric Chopin
Op. 41, No. 3

**Allegretto**

*à Monsieur Etienne Witwicki*

# MAZURKA
### in C-sharp minor

Frédéric Chopin
Op. 41, No. 4

*à Monsieur Léon Szmitkowski*

# MAZURKA

in G Major

Frédéric Chopin
Op. 50, No. 1

*à Monsieur Léon Szmitkowski*

# MAZURKA
in A-flat Major

Frédéric Chopin
Op. 50, No. 2

*à Monsieur Léon Szmitkowski*

# MAZURKA
in C-sharp minor

Frédéric Chopin
Op. 50, No. 3

à Mademoiselle C. Maberly

# MAZURKA
in B Major

Frédéric Chopin
Op. 56, No. 1

Allegro non tanto

**Tempo I**

*à Mademoiselle C. Maberly*

# MAZURKA
## in C Major

Frédéric Chopin
Op. 56, No. 2

à Mademoiselle C. Maberly

# MAZURKA

in C minor

Frédéric Chopin
Op. 56, No. 3

# MAZURKA
## in A minor

Frédéric Chopin
Op. 59, No. 1

# MAZURKA
## in A-flat Major

Frédéric Chopin
Op. 59, No. 2

295

# MAZURKA

in F-sharp minor

Frédéric Chopin
Op. 59, No. 3

*à Madame la Comtesse L. Czosnowska*

# MAZURKA

## in B Major

Frédéric Chopin
Op. 63, No. 1

à Madame la Comtesse L. Czosnowska

# MAZURKA
in F minor

Frédéric Chopin
Op. 63, No. 2

*à Madame la Comtesse L. Czosnowska*

# MAZURKA
in C-sharp minor

Frédéric Chopin
Op. 63, No. 3

# MAZURKA
## in G Major

Frédéric Chopin
Op. 67, No. 1
(Posthumous)

# MAZURKA

## in G minor

Frédéric Chopin
Op. 67, No. 2
(Posthumous)

# MAZURKA
### in C Major

Frédéric Chopin
Op. 67, No. 3
(Posthumous)

# MAZURKA

in A minor

Frédéric Chopin
Op. 67, No. 4
(Posthumous)

Moderato animato (♩ = 138)

# MAZURKA
in C Major

Frédéric Chopin
Op. 68, No. 1
(Posthumous)

# MAZURKA
### in A minor

Frédéric Chopin
Op. 68, No. 2
(Posthumous)

# MAZURKA
### in F Major

Frédéric Chopin
Op. 68, No. 3
(Posthumous)

Allegro, ma non troppo (♩ = 132)

# MAZURKA
## in F minor

Frédéric Chopin
Op. 68, No. 4
(Posthumous)

*D. C. al segno senza fine*

# MAZURKA
## in G Major

Frédéric Chopin
KK. IIa, No. 2

*Dal Segno* *

* Play measures 1-8, followed by the Trio.

Trio

*D.C. al Fine*

# MAZURKA
## in B-flat Major

Frédéric Chopin
KK. IIa, No. 3

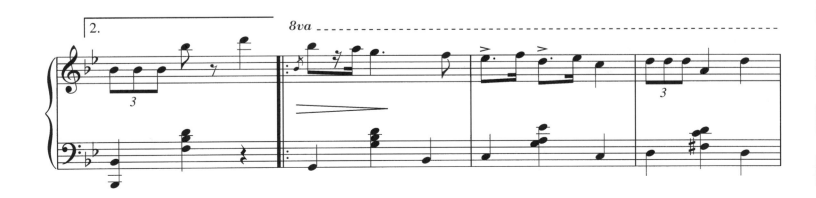

*D.S. al Fine*

# MAZURKA
## in A minor

Frédéric Chopin
KK. IIb, No. 4

*poco cresc.*

# MAZURKA
### in A minor

Frédéric Chopin
KK. IIb, No. 5

# MAZURKA
## in B-flat Major

Frédéric Chopin
KK. IVb, No. 1

stretto

**Fine**

Trio

*D.S. al Fine*

# MAZURKA
## in D Major

Frédéric Chopin
KK. IVb, No. 2

Trio

# MAZURKA
## in A-flat Major

Frédéric Chopin
KK. IVb, No. 4

# MAZURKA
## in C Major

Frédéric Chopin
KK IVb, No. 3

# Nocturnes

*à Madame Camilla Pleyel*

# NOCTURNE
in B-flat minor

Frédéric Chopin
Op. 9, No. 1

Larghetto (♩ = 116)

*à Madame Camilla Pleyel*

# NOCTURNE
## in E-flat Major

Frédéric Chopin
Op. 9, No. 2

*à Madame Camilla Pleyel*

# NOCTURNE
in B Major

Frédéric Chopin
Op. 9, No. 3

*à Monsieur Ferdinand Hiller*

# NOCTURNE
in F Major

Frédéric Chopin
Op. 15, No. 1

*à Monsieur Ferdinand Hiller*

# NOCTURNE
## in F-sharp Major

Frédéric Chopin
Op. 15, No. 2

*à Mr. Ferdinand Hiller*

# NOCTURNE
in G minor

Frédéric Chopin
Op. 15, No. 3

378

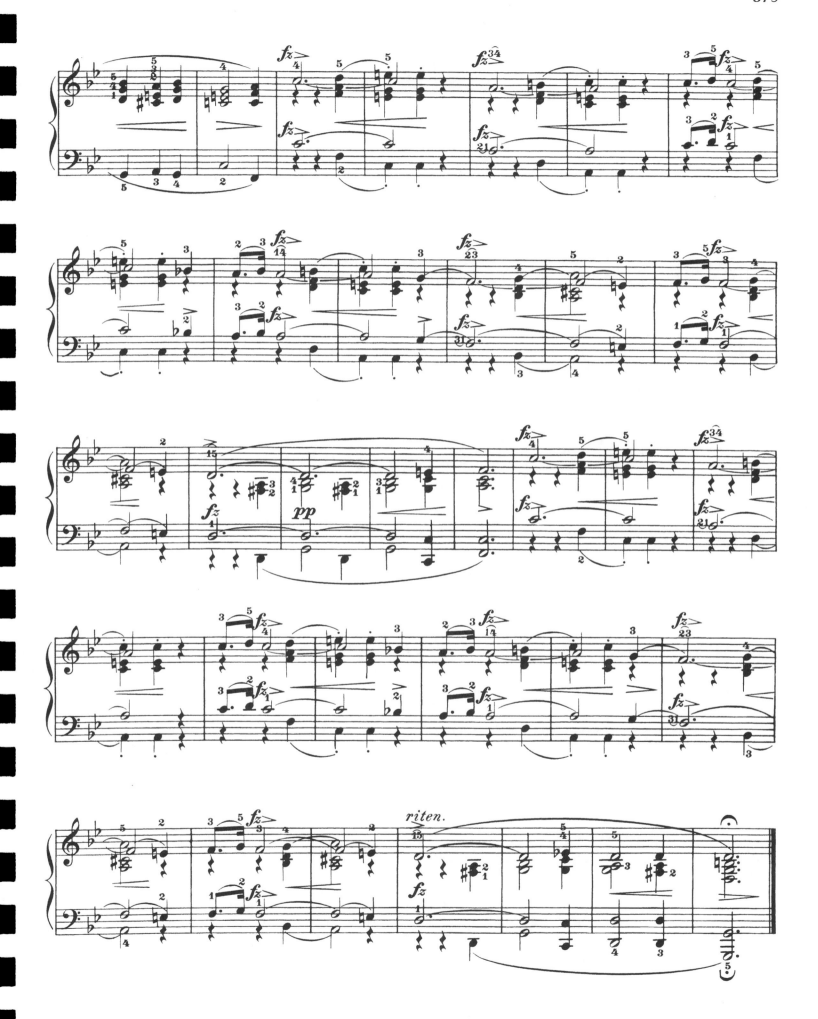

*à Madame la Comtesse d'Appony*

# NOCTURNE

in C-sharp minor

Frédéric Chopin
Op. 27, No. 1

*à Madame la Comtesse d'Appony*

# NOCTURNE
### in D-flat Major

Frédéric Chopin
Op. 27, No. 2

à Madame la Baronne de Billing, née de Courbonne

# NOCTURNE
## in B Major

Frédéric Chopin
Op. 32, No. 1

*à Madame la Baronne de Billing, née de Courbonne*

# NOCTURNE
### in A-flat Major

Frédéric Chopin
Op. 32, No. 2

# NOCTURNE
## in G minor

Frédéric Chopin
Op. 37, No. 1

# NOCTURNE
## in G Major

Frédéric Chopin
Op. 37, No. 2

*) Dieser Takt ist in der Klindworth Ausgabe weggelassen.

à Mademoiselle Laura Duperré

# NOCTURNE
in C minor

Frédéric Chopin
Op. 48, No. 1

*à Mademoiselle Laura Duperré*

# NOCTURNE
in F-sharp minor

Frédéric Chopin
Op. 48, No. 2

Klindworth:

à Mademoiselle J. W. Stirling

# NOCTURNE
### in F minor

Frédéric Chopin
Op. 55, No. 1

*à Mademoiselle J. W. Stirling*

# NOCTURNE
## in E-flat Major

Frédéric Chopin
Op. 55, No. 2

Lento sostenuto

à Mademoiselle R. de Könneritz

# NOCTURNE

in B Major

Frédéric Chopin
Op. 62, No. 1

*à Mademoiselle R. de Könneritz*

# NOCTURNE
## in E Major

Frédéric Chopin
Op. 62, No. 2

# NOCTURNE
## in C minor

Frédéric Chopin
KK. IVb, No. 8

**Andante sostenuto**

# NOCTURNE
## in E minor

Frédéric Chopin
Op. 72, No. 1
(Posthumous)

# NOCTURNE
## in C-sharp minor

Frédéric Chopin
KK. Anh. Ia, No. 6

# Polonaises

*à M. J. Dessauer*

# POLONAISE
in C-sharp minor

Frédéric Chopin
Op. 26, No. 1

**Allegro appassionato**

Fine.

Polonaise da Capo al Fine

*à M. J. Dessauer*

# POLONAISE
in E-flat minor

Frédéric Chopin
Op. 26, No. 2

*) While Mme. Rubio was studying this 2ⁿᵈ Polonaise with Chopin, he wrote with his own hand in her copy (in divergence from the books of the other pupils) at this passage and its repetition, a ♮ instead of a ♭ before D.

*à M. Jules Fontana*

# POLONAISE
in A Major

Frédéric Chopin
Op. 40, No. 1

Allegro con brio

*à M. Jules Fontana*

# POLONAISE
### in C minor

Frédéric Chopin
Op. 40, No. 2

*à Madame la Princesse Charles de Beavau*

# POLONAISE
in F-sharp minor

Frédéric Chopin
Op. 44

Doppio movimento: (Tempo di Mazurka)

sotto voce

**Tempo I** *(di Polacca)*

*à M. Auguste Leo*

# POLONAISE
in A-flat Major

Frédéric Chopin
Op. 53

502

*à Madame A. Veyret*

# POLONAISE
in A-flat Major

Frédéric Chopin
Op. 61

Allegro maestoso

# POLONAISE
### in D minor

Frédéric Chopin
Op. 71, No. 1
(Posthumous)

# POLONAISE
### in B-flat Major

Frédéric Chopin
Op. 71, No. 2
(Posthumous)

Allegro, ma non troppo (♩ = 92)

# POLONAISE
## in F minor

Frédéric Chopin
Op. 71, No. 3
(Posthumous)

*à Mademoiselle la Comtesse Victoire Skarbek*

# POLONAISE

in G minor

Frédéric Chopin
KK. IIa, No. 1

Trio

*Polonaise D.C. al Fine*

# POLONAISE
## in B-flat Major

Frédéric Chopin
KK. IVa, No. 1

*Polonaise D.C. al Fine*

*à M. A. Zywny*

# POLONAISE
in A-flat Major

Frédéric Chopin
KK. IVa, No. 2

Trio

*Polonaise D.C. al Fine*

*à M. G. Kolberg*

# POLONAISE
### in B-flat minor

Frédéric Chopin
KK. IVa, No. 5

Trio

*Polonaise D.C. al Fine*

*à Madame Du-Pont*

# POLONAISE
in G-sharp minor

Frédéric Chopin
KK. IVa, No. 3

# POLONAISE
## in G-flat Major

Frédéric Chopin
KK. IVa, No. 8

D.C. al Fine

# Préludes

*à J. C. Kessler*

# PRÉLUDE

in C Major

Frédéric Chopin
Op. 28, No. 1

*à J. C. Kessler*

# PRÉLUDE

in A minor

Frédéric Chopin
Op. 28, No. 2

*à J. C. Kessler*

# PRÉLUDE
## in G Major

Frédéric Chopin
Op. 28, No. 3

\*) Carl Tausig, who had a marked preference for a stretchedout position of the fingers, used the following fingering:

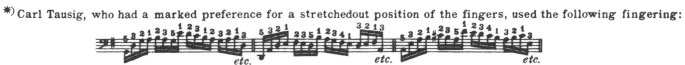

*à J. C. Kessler*

# PRÉLUDE
## in E minor

Frédéric Chopin
Op. 28, No. 4

*à J. C. Kessler*

# PRÉLUDE
in D Major

Frédéric Chopin
Op. 28, No. 5

**Allegro molto**

*à J. C. Kessler*

# PRÉLUDE
## in B minor

Frédéric Chopin
Op. 28, No. 6

*à J. C. Kessler*

# PRÉLUDE
### in A Major

Frédéric Chopin
Op. 28, No. 7

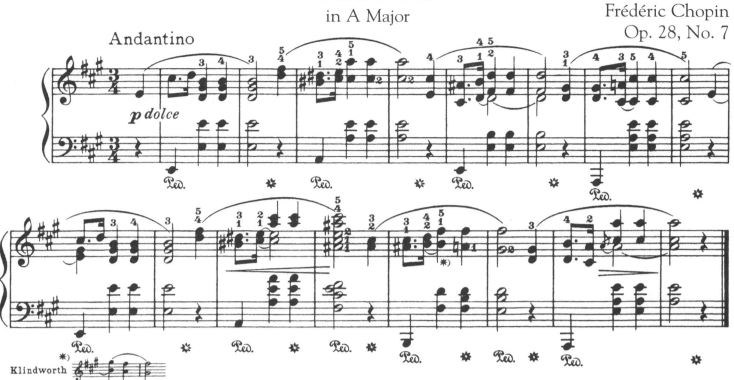

*à J. C. Kessler*

# PRÉLUDE
### in F-sharp minor

Frédéric Chopin
Op. 28, No. 8

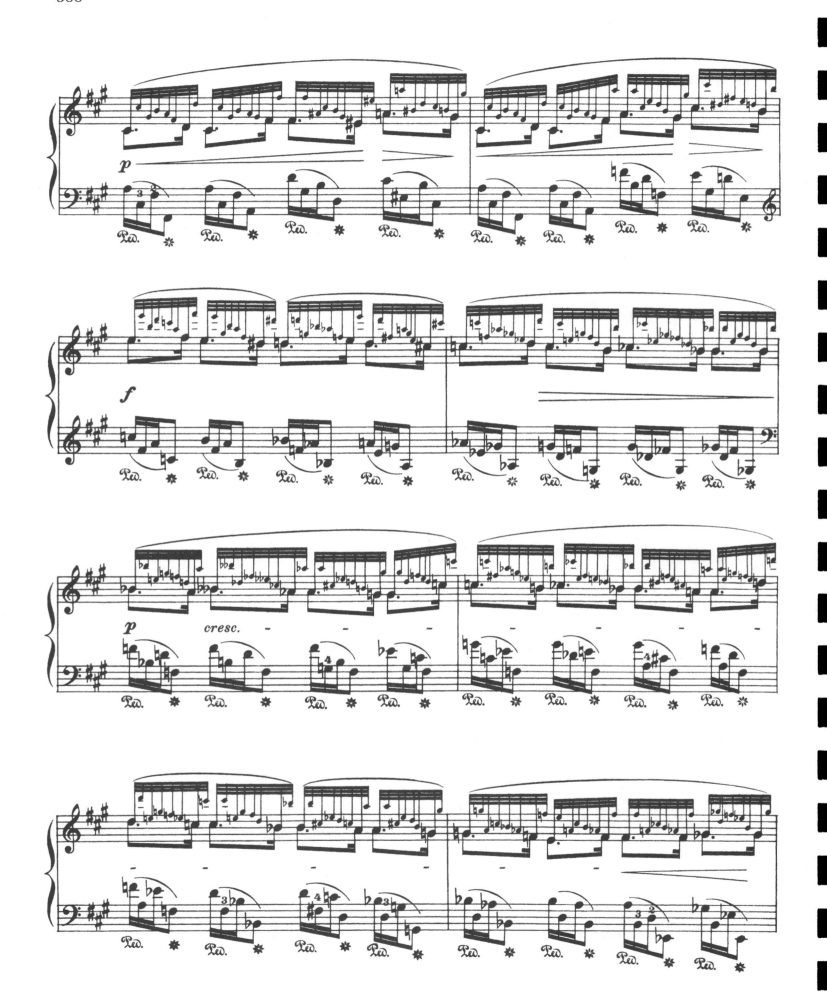

589

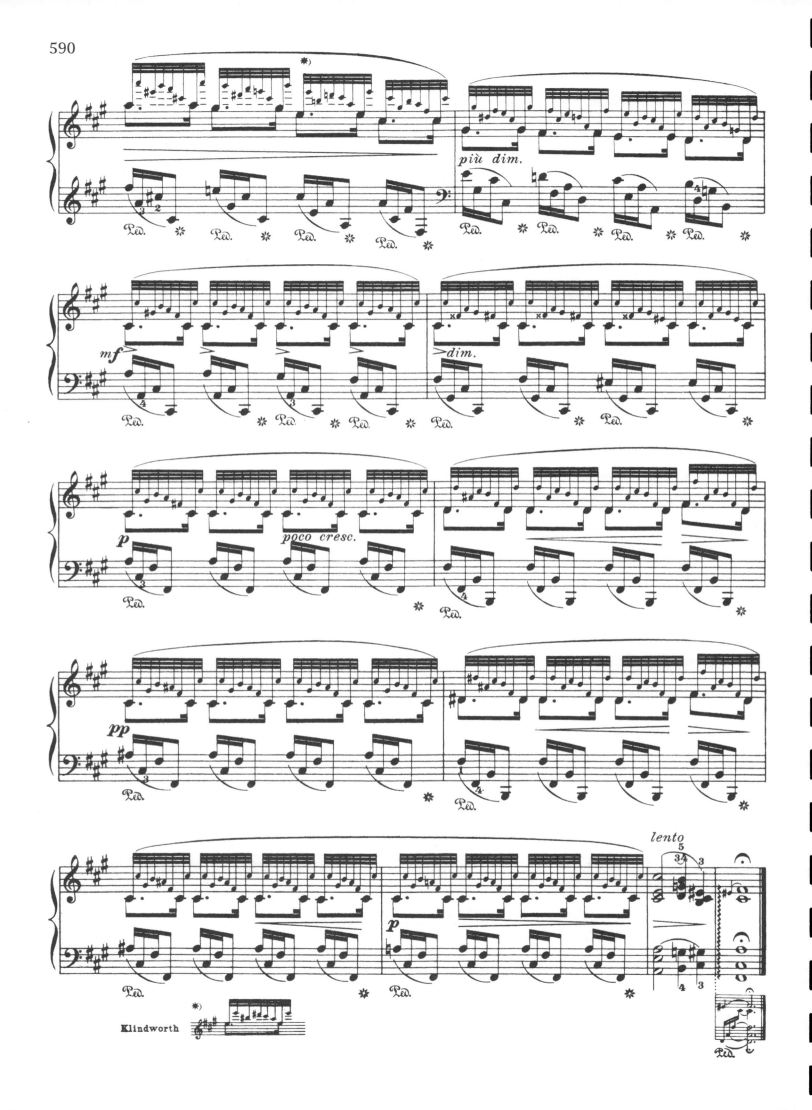

Klindworth

*à J. C. Kessler*

# PRÉLUDE
### in E Major

Frédéric Chopin
Op. 28, No. 9

*) Scholz:

*à J. C. Kessler*

# PRÉLUDE
in C-sharp minor

Frédéric Chopin
Op. 28, No. 10

Allegro molto

*à J. C. Kessler*

# PRÉLUDE
in B Major

Frédéric Chopin
Op. 28, No. 11

à J. C. Kessler

# PRÉLUDE
in G-sharp minor

Frédéric Chopin
Op. 28, No. 12

*à J. C. Kessler*

# PRÉLUDE
## in F-sharp Major

Frédéric Chopin
Op. 28, No. 13

*à J. C. Kessler*

# PRÉLUDE
in E-flat minor

Frédéric Chopin
Op. 28, No. 14

**Allegro**

*à J. C. Kessler*

# PRÉLUDE
## in D-flat Major

Frédéric Chopin
Op. 28, No. 15

*à C. Kessler*

# PRÉLUDE
in B-flat minor

Frédéric Chopin
Op. 28, No. 16

**Presto con fuoco**

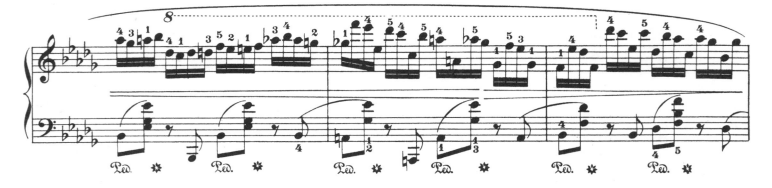

Klindworth:

*à J. C. Kessler*

# PRÉLUDE
in A-flat Major

Frédéric Chopin
Op. 28, No. 17

à J. C. Kessler

# PRÉLUDE
## in F minor

Frédéric Chopin
Op. 28, No. 18

Allegro molto
*agitato*

Klindworth:

*à J. C. Kessler*

# PRÉLUDE
in E-flat Major

Frédéric Chopin
Op. 28, No. 19

*à J. C. Kessler*

# PRÉLUDE
### in C minor

Frédéric Chopin
Op. 28, No. 20

*à J. C. Kessler*

# PRÉLUDE
### in B-flat Major

Frédéric Chopin
Op. 28, No. 21

à J. C. Kessler

# PRÉLUDE
## in G minor

Frédéric Chopin
Op. 28, No. 22

*à J. C. Kessler*

# PRÉLUDE
in F Major

Frédéric Chopin
Op. 28, No. 23

*à J. C. Kessler*

# PRÉLUDE
## in D minor

Frédéric Chopin
Op. 28, No. 24

**Allegro appassionato**

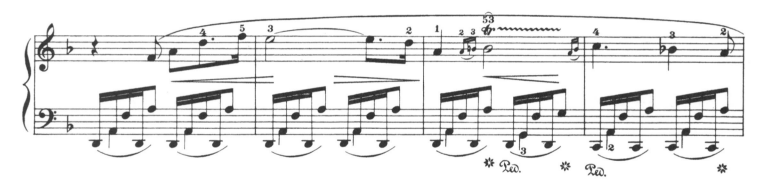

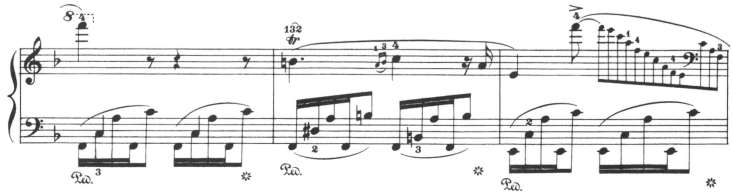

*à Mademoiselle la Princesse Élisabeth Czernicheff*

# PRÉLUDE

in C-sharp minor

Frédéric Chopin
Op. 45

*à mon ami Pierre Wolff*

# PRÉLUDE
in A-flat Major

Frédéric Chopin
KK. IVb, No. 7

**Presto con leggierezza**

# WALTZES

*à Laura Harsford*

# GRAND VALSE BRILLANTE
in E-flat Major

Frédéric Chopin
Op. 18

639

*à Mademoiselle de Thun Hohenstein*

# VALSE BRILLANTE
## in A-flat Major

Frédéric Chopin
Op. 34, No. 1

*à Madame G. d'Ivry*

# VALSE BRILLANTE
## in A minor

Frédéric Chopin
Op. 34, No. 2

*à Mademoiselle A. d'Eichthal*

# VALSE BRILLANTE
## in F Major

Frédéric Chopin
Op. 34, No. 3

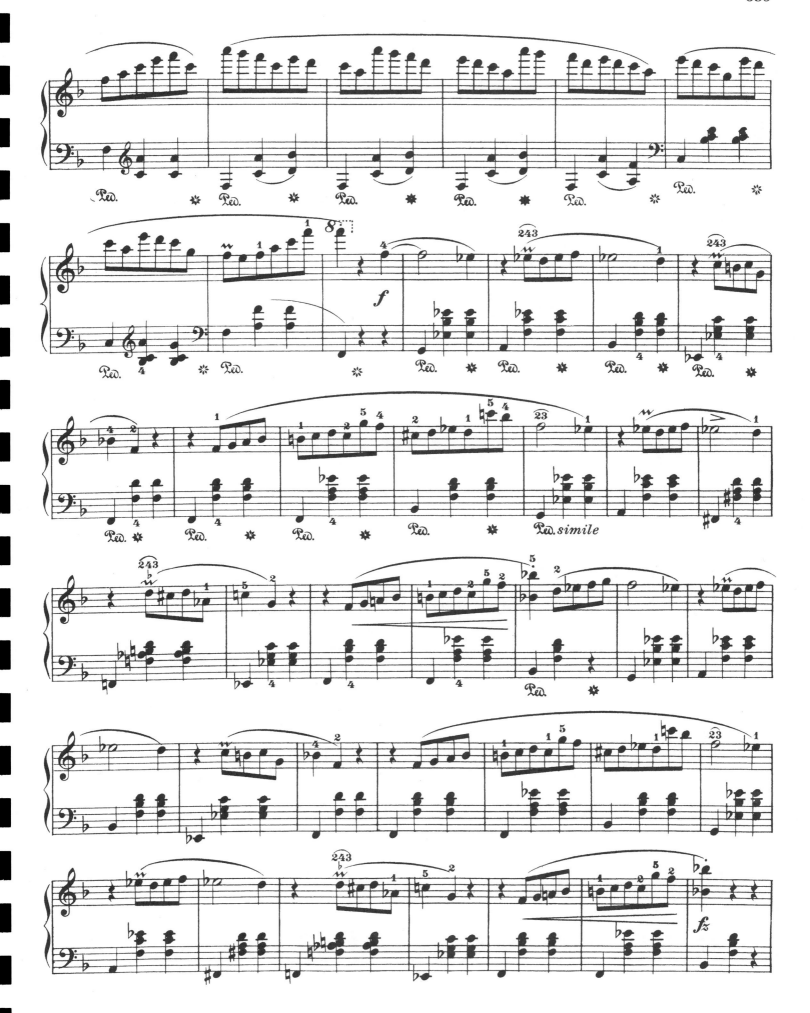

# WALTZ
## in A-flat Major

Frédéric Chopin
Op. 42

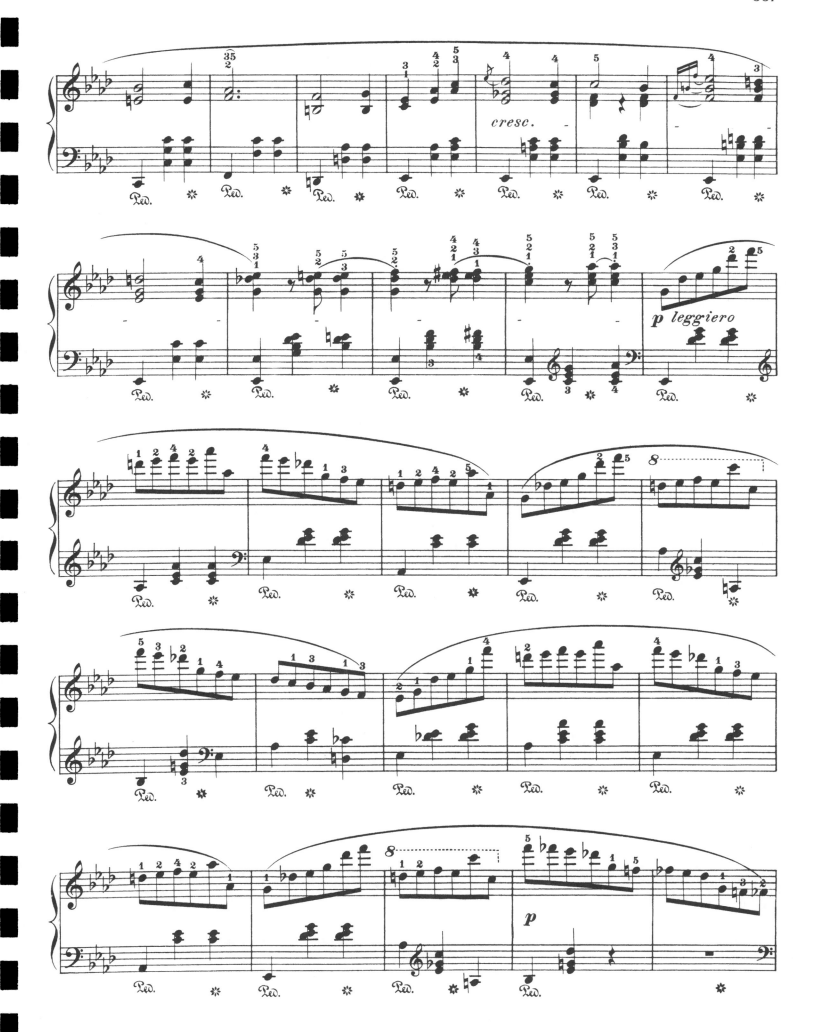

*à Madame la Comtesse Delphine Potocka*

# WALTZ
### in D-flat Major

Frédéric Chopin
Op. 64, No. 1

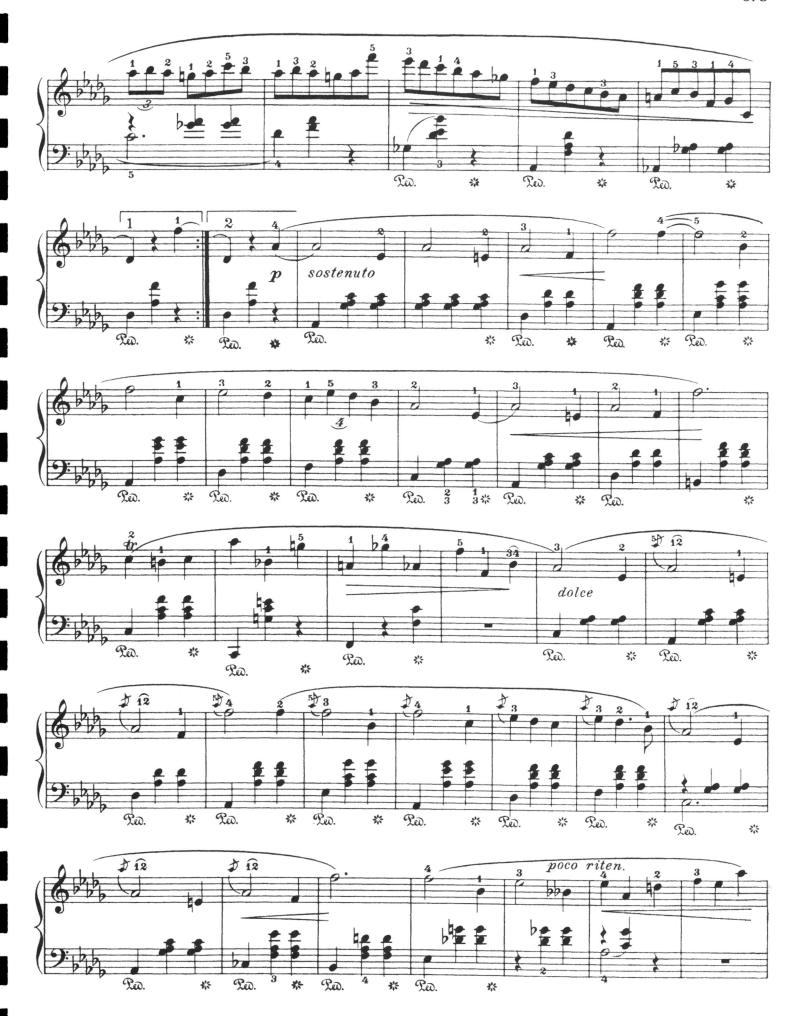

*à Madame Nathaniel de Rothschild*

# WALTZ
## in C-sharp minor

Frédéric Chopin
Op. 64, No. 2

Klindworth:

*à la Comtesse Katharina Bronicka*

# WALTZ
## in A-flat Major

Frédéric Chopin
Op. 64, No. 3

Moderato

poco a poco accel. al fine

# WALTZ
## in A-flat Major

Frédéric Chopin
Op. 69, No. 1
(Posthumous)

# WALTZ
## in B minor

Frédéric Chopin
Op. 69, No. 2
(Posthumous)

# WALTZ
## in G-flat Major

Frédéric Chopin
Op. 70, No. 1
(Posthumous)

# WALTZ
## in D-flat Major

Frédéric Chopin
Op. 70, No. 3
(Posthumous)

# WALTZ
## in F minor

Frédéric Chopin
Op. 70, No. 2
(Posthumous)

# WALTZ
## in E Major

Frédéric Chopin
KK. IVa, No. 12

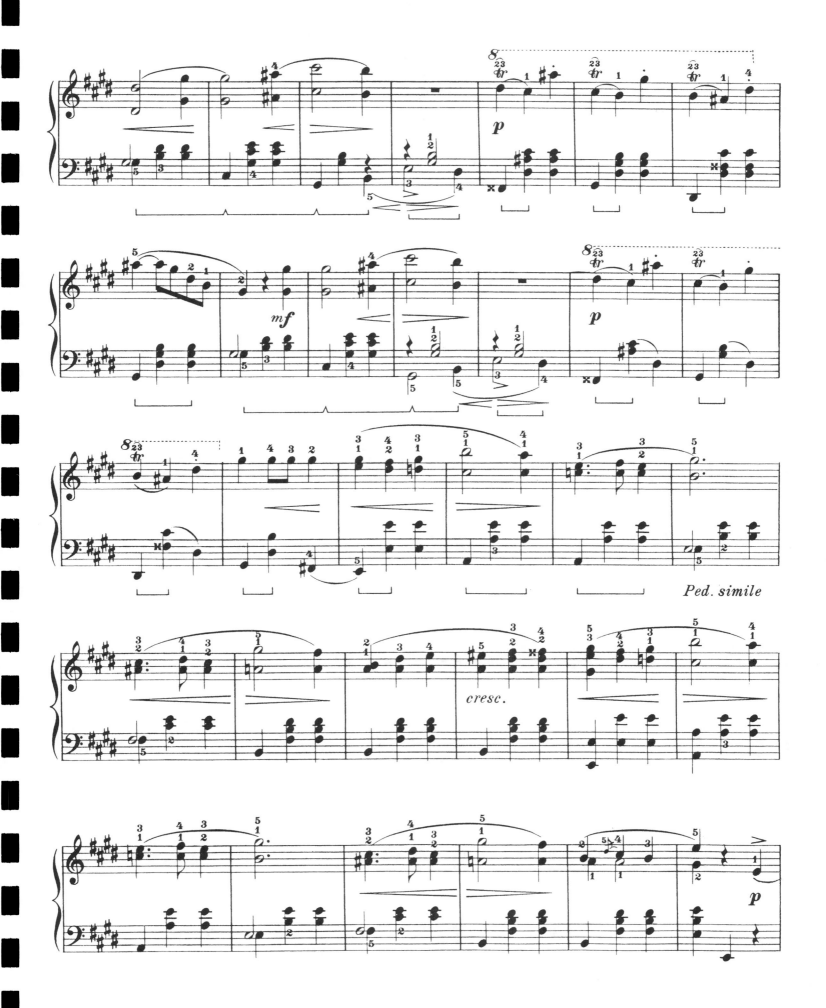

# WALTZ
## in A-flat Major

Frédéric Chopin
KK. IVa, No. 13

*Fine*

*D.C. al Fine*

# WALTZ
## in E-flat Major

Frédéric Chopin
KK. IVa, No. 14

# WALTZ
## in E-flat Major

Frédéric Chopin
KK. IVb, No. 10

**Sostenuto**

# WALTZ
## in E minor

Frédéric Chopin
KK. IVa, No. 15

# WALTZ
## in A minor

Frédéric Chopin
KK. IVb, No. 11

**Allegretto**